TOP 50 QUESTIONS

Rocks and Minerals

SEYMOUR SIMON

SCHOLASTIC INC.

New York   Toronto   London   Auckland   Sydney
Mexico City   New Delhi   Hong Kong   Buenos Aires

To Miriam and Bernie's grandkids:
Michael, Daniel (DD), Max, Silas, and Ruby

Acknowledgments

Special thanks to my superb editor, Jenne Abramowitz. Thanks also to Kevin Callahan for his excellent design and to Karen Brooks and Elizabeth Van Houten for their skillful copyediting. The author is grateful to David Reuther for his editorial and design suggestions, as well as his enthusiasm for this project. Also, many thanks to Gina Shaw at Scholastic Inc., for her extraordinary support throughout the publication of the "Top 50 Questions" series.

Photo Credits

Front cover and page 11 (top): © Doug Martin/Photo Researchers, Inc.; back cover: © Carl Frank/ Photo Researchers, Inc.; page 1: © Keith Kent/Photo Researchers, Inc.; pages 3, 10, 14, and 16 (top): E. R. Degginger/Dembinsky Photo Associates; page 4: © Wayne Scherr/Photo Researchers, Inc.; page 5: © Alfred Pasieka/Photo Researchers, Inc.; page 6: © Simon Fraser/Photo Researchers, Inc.; page 7: © John Mead/Photo Researchers, Inc.; pages 8, 11 (bottom), and 18 (top): © Joyce Photographics/Photo Researchers, Inc.; page 9: © Bourseiller/Durieux/Photo Researchers, Inc.; page 12: © George Bernard/Photo Researchers, Inc.; page 13: © Joe Sroka/ Dembinsky Photo Associates; pages 14–15: Adam Jones/Photo Researchers, Inc.; page 15: © Dominique Braud/Dembinsky Photo Associates; page 16 (bottom): © Brenda Tharp/ Photo Researchers, Inc.; page 17 (top): © Kenneth Murray/Photo Researchers, Inc.; page 17 (bottom): © Aaron Haupt/Photo Researchers, Inc.; page 18 (bottom): © Charles D. Winters/Photo Researchers, Inc.; page 19 (top): © Patti McConville/Dembinsky Photo Associates; pages 19 (bottom), 23 (bottom), 24 (bottom), and 25 (top): © Mark A. Schneider/Dembinsky Photo Associates.; page 20: © David Grossman/Photo Researchers, Inc.; pages 21, 23 (top), and 30: © Lawrence Lawry/ Photo Researchers, Inc.; page 22 (top): © Richard Green/Photo Researchers, Inc.; page 22 (bottom): © Francois Gohier/Photo Researchers, Inc.; page 24 (top): © Dirk Wiersma/Photo Researchers, Inc.; page 25 (bottom): © E. R. Degginger/Photo Researchers, Inc.; pages 26 and 27: © DEA/A. Rizzi/ Getty Images; page 29 (top): © Mark A. Schneider/Photo Researchers, Inc.; page 29 (bottom): © Jacana/Photo Researchers, Inc.

ISBN-13: 978-0-439-79599-9
ISBN-10: 0-439-79599-0

12 11 10 9 8 7 6 5 4   9 10 11 12 13/0

Printed in the U.S.A.
First printing, November 2008

INTRODUCTION

① What are minerals?

Minerals are hard, nonliving materials. They are made of basic substances called elements. There are ninety-two natural elements. There are more than three thousand known minerals. Of these, about thirty form rocks.

Calcite

② What are rocks?

There are thousands of different kinds of rocks. They come in all colors. They can be smooth or rough, shiny or dull. Rocks are made of a mixture of minerals or other rocks.

3 What do crystals look like?

Crystals are the shapes created as a mineral forms. All crystals of the same mineral look alike. For example, pyrite crystals are always cube shaped. So a mineral can often be identified by the shape of its crystals.

4 How are crystals formed?

Crystals form when liquid rock inside the earth cools slowly and hardens over thousands of years. When rocks don't cool slowly enough, they will not form crystals.

5

⑤ How does water change rocks

Water often comes into contact with rocks in the form of rain, rivers, and oceans. It dissolves and wears away rocks by a process called weathering or erosion. After many years of weathering, small pieces of rocks are worn into grains of sand. Sand can mix with decaying plant and animal matter to become the soil where plants grow.

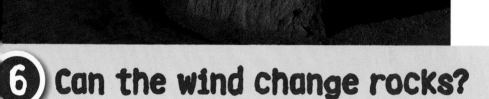

6 Can the wind change rocks?

Wind can also weather rocks. Winds pick up particles of sand and soil and beat them against larger rocks. This can wear away the rocks in the same way water does.

7 What other things can change rocks?

Rocks change as ice freezes and melts. Water seeps into holes and cracks in rocks. When the water freezes, it turns to ice. Ice expands and makes the holes and cracks larger. Rocks can also break down by being heated and cooled, by combining with chemicals in the air and water, by plant growth, and by digging animals.

⑧ Where are rocks found?

Rocks are found on the outer part, or crust, of the earth.

Igneous

Sedimentary

⑨ Are there different types of rocks?

Rocks are usually grouped by the way they are formed. The three main classes of rock are igneous, sedimentary, and metamorphic. Igneous rocks are the first rocks formed on the earth's crust. Sedimentary and metamorphic rocks come from changed igneous rocks.

Metamorphic

⑩ Are new rocks ever created?

New rocks are always being created inside the earth and on its surface. And old rocks are always weathering and changing into different rocks.

IGNEOUS ROCKS

11 What happens when a volcano erupts?

Volcanoes are formed when hot, melted rock inside the earth, called magma, pushes its way up through cracks in the earth's crust. This is called a volcanic eruption. When magma pours forth on the surface in liquid form, it is called lava.

12 How do igneous rocks form?

Igneous rocks are formed from magma under the earth's surface or on its crust. As the magma cools, it hardens into solid rock.

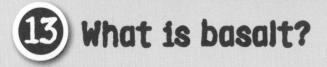

13 What is basalt?

Basalt is a hard, dark gray or black igneous rock. It is formed by the rapid cooling and hardening of lava from a volcano. Basalt is usually fine grained. It is difficult to see individual minerals without a magnifying lens. The ocean floor and volcanic islands, such as Hawaii and Iceland, are mostly made of basalt.

14 Is there a natural volcanic glass?

Obsidian is a rock that's created when lava erupts from a volcano and then cools rapidly without time for crystals to form. Obsidian is usually black, very dark red, or brown, and very smooth. Obsidian is hard and chips easily into thin-edged pieces. Native Americans in the West often used obsidian to make arrowheads and knives.

15 Which rock is full of holes?

Pumice is a pale gray rock that looks like a sponge. It forms from lava while steam and other gases are still bubbling. Pumice is sometimes light enough to float on water. It's so soft you can scratch it with your fingernail.

16 What is the most common igneous rock?

Granite is found all over the world. It's composed of light-colored minerals such as quartz, pink or gray feldspar, and a dark mineral such as mica or hornblende. The dark minerals give granite a speckled look.

17 How do sedimentary rocks form?

The tiny pieces of rocks and minerals that come from weathering are called sediments. They roll down from hills and mountains and are carried along by streams and rivers until they reach low-lying lands or oceans. Over thousands of years, pressure and heat in the earth's crust squeeze and mold the sediments and change them into rocks.

(18) What is sandstone?

Sandstone is made of grains of rock cemented together by other minerals dissolved in water. Sandstone is usually light yellow, tan, gray, or white. If you break off a piece of sandstone, you can feel the grains of sand on the broken edges. Sandstone is often used in buildings and in making glass.

(19) How is limestone different from sandstone?

Limestone is a soft sedimentary rock like sandstone. But it's made of a different mineral, called calcite. Because water rapidly dissolves limestone, caves often form in limestone deposits. Some of the best-known limestone caves in the United States are Luray Caverns in Virginia, Mammoth Cave in Kentucky, and Carlsbad Caverns in New Mexico.

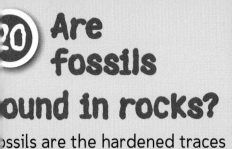

20) Are fossils found in rocks?

ossils are the hardened traces
remains of an animal or plant. They are mainly found in
edimentary rocks such as limestone. Sometimes shells or
npressions of sea animals can be found in a piece of rock.
ome rocks are formed almost entirely from fossils. For
kample, common blackboard chalk is mostly limestone that
made up of the remains of coral animals.

21 What is conglomerate?

Conglomerate is a rock made up of gravel and smooth, rounded pebbles. The pebbles are rounded after being tossed around by waves or running water. Conglomerate is sometimes called pudding stone because it looks like pudding with lumps in it.

22 How is breccia different from conglomerate?

Breccia contains pieces of rock just like conglomerate. But the pieces of rock in breccia are sharp and not smooth or rounded by water.

METAMORPHIC ROCKS

(23) How do metamorphic rocks form?

Metamorphic rocks are changed rocks. They were once igneous or sedimentary rocks that were altered by great heat and pressure within the earth.

(24) What rock is used to make chalkboards?

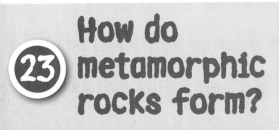

Chalkboards are made from slate. Slate was once a sedimentary rock called shale. Heat and pressure make it much harder and smoother than shale. Slate splits into sheets that are used for chalkboards, roof tiles, and floor tiles. Slate may be black, gray, red, green, or purple.

25 What is quartzite?

Quartzite is a hard rock in which all the empty spaces in sandstone have been filled with quartz crystals. The crystals give the rock a glassy appearance.

26 What rock glitters in the sun?

Schist is a rock often named after its most abundant mineral. Mica schist is a common type that sparkles because it contains flakes of a shiny mineral called mica. Mica can be split into thin, almost transparent, layers. Because it is resistant to heat, mica is sometimes used instead of glass in stove windows.

Where does coal come from?

Coal is mostly made of the element carbon from the remains of tropical and subtropical plants that covered parts of North America, Europe, and Asia. It was formed over many millions of years. The plant material was buried in the ground and compressed into a sedimentary rock called peat. Over time, peat changed into coal. Different kinds of coal are burned for heat and electricity.

28 What is gneiss?

Gneiss is metamorphic rock that usually has large crystals and a banded appearance. Gneiss often has alternating bands of mica and hornblende.

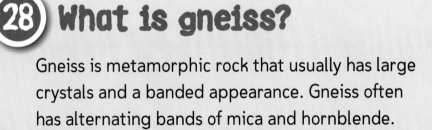

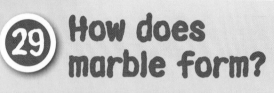

29 How does marble form?

Very high temperatures within the earth may change limestone into a rock called marble. Marble is a soft rock. You can scratch it with a knife. Pure marble is white but chemicals may color it in swirls and patterns of color. Marble is often used in buildings and sculpture.

30 What are some other metamorphic rocks?

Slate can sometimes become hot enough to form a new rock called hornfels. Schists and gneisses can be banded with quartz, feldspar, and granite. Schists also can contain garnets and other mineral crystals.

(31) What are diamonds?

Diamonds are a crystal form of the element carbon. They are the hardest known substance. Pure diamonds are colorless and used in jewelry. Imperfect, or industrial, diamonds are used for cutting, drilling, and grinding.

(32) Can diamonds be created?

Real diamonds rarely occur in nature. Synthetic diamonds are man-made. They are produced by subjecting carbon to very high temperatures and pressures.

33 What are emeralds, rubies, and sapphires?

Green emeralds, red rubies, and blue sapphires are minerals called gemstones. Gemstones are valued for their beauty, hardness, color, and rarity. The most precious gems are single large crystals that are cut, polished, and used to make jewelry and other fine objects.

34 Is amber a mineral?

Amber is a sticky resin or sap that once dripped from trees in ancient forests and then hardened over millions of years. Although not a mineral, amber is used to make jewelry. It often contains bits and pieces of plants, insects, spiders, and other small organisms.

35 What is turquoise?

Turquoise is a blue-green mineral that is used to make jewelry. Turquoise was one of the first gems to be mined.

36 Are there other precious stones?

There are many precious and semiprecious minerals and stones. Some of these are opal, agate, jade, lapis, topaz, amethyst, tourmaline, garnet, and zircon. They come in many different colors and are used to make jewelry and other fine objects.

Amethyst

23

37 Why is gold valuable?

Gold is found in nuggets or mixed with other rocks in specks too small to see. It has been a highly prized mineral throughout history because of its beautiful appearance. Gold is most often used to make jewelry. But it's also used in dentistry, in computer and electrical circuitry, and in many other industrial products.

38 What is fool's gold?

Iron pyrite is a mineral often called fool's gold. Miners sometimes mistook it for real gold because of its brassy yellow color.

Where does silver come from?

39

Silver has been used for jewelry since ancient times. Silver is often found mixed together with lead and other minerals in rocks. It's the least expensive precious metal, often worth less than 1/50 the price of gold.

Are there other precious metals?

40

The most common precious metals are gold and silver. However, other metals are also valuable. Platinum is worth about twice the price of gold. Rhodium is even more expensive than platinum, valued about eight times the price of gold.

Platinum

41 Are you a rock hound?

Have you ever bent down and picked up a rock from the ground? Perhaps you put the rock in your pocket and brought it home or to school. If you did, you are on your way to becoming a rock hound. Rock hounds are people who enjoy finding and collecting rocks and minerals. They learn how to identify them. Rock hounds like to get out and explore the world of rocks and minerals all around them.

42 How can you start a rock collection?

You can collect rocks from your own neighborhood or make collecting trips to near or distant places. You can also trade or buy rocks from all over the world.

43 How should you store your collection?

Each rock or mineral should be identified and labeled. Wash each one carefully in water and wait until it dries before you try to identify it. Label each specimen with a number written in ink on a small piece of adhesive tape. Put the same number on a card or in a computer file and write down any information you know about it.

You can store most rocks in small cardboard boxes. Use cardboard to separate each rock. Try using egg cartons for smaller specimens. Small crystals and delicate minerals need more care. You can keep them on a bed of cotton in small plastic boxes.

44 How can you display your collection?

You may want to keep some of your interesting-looking rocks and minerals on display. Most will look best if you paste them in a small plastic cube or box. You can mount larger specimens on blocks of wood that you can paint to make more attractive. You can also use pieces of polystyrene cut to the right size.

45 How can you identify rocks?

Most of the common rocks you will find are described and pictured in this book in chapters 2, 3, and 4. For unusual specimens, use a rock-collecting guidebook or go to a natural history museum that has a rock and mineral collection. Many Web sites have photo galleries and searchable guides to rocks and minerals.

46 What are the best ways to identify a mineral?

Identifying a mineral can be difficult. One clue may not be enough. Here are some ways to gather information:

- Color—Color is easy to see, but not too dependable. The same mineral can be many different colors. For example, quartz can be clear, rose, violet, smoky, milky, green, black, or banded.
- Streak—You can streak a mineral by rubbing it against a piece of unglazed porcelain, such as the back of a bathroom tile. The streak of the mineral will always be the same color.
- Luster—The way the mineral shines in light is called luster. Minerals can have lusters that look metallic, glassy, silky, waxy, greasy, or dull.
- Cleavage or fracture—How does the mineral break?

47 What is the Mohs Scale?

The Mohs Scale charts the relative hardness of minerals. Minerals on this scale will scratch any other mineral with a lower number. Your fingernail (2.5) can scratch talc (1) and gypsum (2). A steel knife (5.5) can scratch apatite (4). Glass (5.5) can be scratched by quartz (7).

Mohs Number	Rock Type
1	Talc
2	Gypsum
3	Calcite
4	Fluorite
5	Apatite
6	Feldspar
7	Quartz
8	Topaz
9	Corundum
10	Diamond

(48) What are the hardest minerals and rocks in the world?

Diamonds are the hardest mineral. They are four times harder than the next hardest minerals, sapphires and rubies. There is no single hardest rock. The hardest are those that contain lots of quartz.

(49) What rock-collecting tools can you use?

Wear sturdy clothing and shoes. Take along a bag made of a strong material that has a strap or a handle. Bring along some newspaper or grocery bags to wrap each specimen. Carry a notebook and write down the number of the specimen (starting with 1), where you found it, the date, and the kinds of rocks found around it. Mark the specimen with a marking pen or with adhesive tape. You can also bring a magnifying lens to look at small crystals.

(50) What are some more fun things for rock hounds to do?

- Join a rock-hound club. Meet and talk to others that love rocks and minerals. Ask your teacher or a natural history museum for suggestions on finding a club near you.
- Polish rocks and minerals to a shiny smoothness with a rock tumbler. You can find rock tumblers in hobby stores or on the Internet.
- Use your finest specimens to make jewelry. Many hobby stores sell mountings for rings and bracelets.

INDEX

amber 22

basalt 10

breccia 16

carbon 19, 21

caves 14

coal 19

collecting 26–28, 31

conglomerate 16

crust 8, 9, 13

crystals 5, 18, 20, 21

diamond 21, 29, 30

elements 3

emerald 22

erosion 6–7

fool's gold (iron pyrite) 5, 24

fossils 15, 22

gemstones 21–23

gold 24, 25

granite 12, 20

gneiss 19, 20

igneous rocks 8, 9–12, 17

jewelry 21–25, 31

lava (and magma) 9–11

limestone 14, 15, 20

marble 20

metals 24–25

metamorphic rocks 8, 17–20

mica 18, 19, 29

Mohs Scale 29

obsidian 11

platinum 25

pumice 11

quartz 12, 20, 28, 29, 30

quartzite 18

rhodium 25

ruby 22

sandstone 14, 18

sapphire 22

schist 18, 20

sedimentary rocks 8, 13–16, 17, 19

silver 25

slate 17, 20

turquoise 23

volcanoes 9–11

weathering 6–7